The New Sabin

Index to Entries 15804-17945

The New Sabin;

Books Described by Joseph Sabin and His

Successors, Now Described Again on the

Basis of Examination of Originals,

and Fully Indexed by Title, Subject,

Joint Authors, and Institutions and Agencies.

by

Lawrence S. Thompson

Index to Entries 15804-17945

The Whitston Publishing Company
Troy, New York

1980

Library of Congress Catalog Card Number 73-85960

ISBN 0-87875-183-1

Printed in the United States of America

1

3

Aveson, Robert, 16485
Aviaries, 17666
The awakening of the desert,
15987
Aztlan, 17494

Baca, Eleuterio, tr.,
17451
The backbone of Nebraska,
17165
The backwoodsman, 17687
Bade, William Frederic,
1871-, ed., 17245
Bailey, Joseph Weidon,
1863-1929, 16220
Bailey, Mary F., 16164
Bailey, Mrs. Nellie C.
(Benthusen), b. 1862,
16873
Baker, Edward Dickenson,
1811-1861, 16936
Balestier, Joseph Neree,
ed., 17477
Ball's Bluff, Battle of,
1861, 16936
Ballew, Stephen Morris,
16430
El bandido chileno Joaquín
Murieta en California,
16841
The banditti of the prairies,
16014
Baptists - New England,
17756
Baptists - Oregon, 16517
Baptists - Texas, 17838
Baraboo, Wis., 15848
Barker, Eugene Campbell,
1874-, ed., 16892
Barreiro, Antonio, 17392
The barren ground of northern
Canada, 17389
Barrett, Jay Amos, 1865-,
ed., 17260
Barrows, Willard, 1806-1868,
15924
Bartleson, John, 16926
Baskin, O. L. & co., Chicago

pub., 16782
Bastrop Co., Tex. - Biog.,
16780
Baughman, the Oklahoma
scout, 15941
Baumbardt, B. R. & co.,
16877
Beadle, John Hanson, 1840-
1897, ed., 16751
Beale, Edward Fitzgerlad,
16015
Bear flag battalion, 16844
Bear flag party, 16845
Bear Lake Co., Id., 17762
Beating back, 16888
Beatty, Bessie, 17882
Beauties of California,
16650
Beaver (Steamship), 17076
Beaverhead Co., Mont. -
Hist., 17291
Beck, Richard, ed., 17737
Behnke, Julius Camillus, 1859-,
comp. and tr., 17007
Belden, Josiah, 16926
Belleville, Ill., 16754
Bemis, Katherine Isabel,
jt. author, 16807
The bench and bar of Texas,
17074
Bender family, 16883
The Benders in Kansas,
16883
Bennet, Isaac, 1803?-1856,
15902
Benton, Thomas Hart, 1782-
1858, 16554
The Bering sea arbitration,
15972
Beschke, William, comp.,
15810
Biddle, Nicholas, 1786-1844,
17030
Bidwell, John, 1819-1900,
15963, 16926, 17533
Big Bend country, 17032
Big Hole Valley, Mont., 17291
Big Horn expedition, 17197
Big Horn mountains, 17871

4

Big Horn region, 17683
Bill Jones of Paradise
   Valley, Oklahoma, 16134
Billy Le Roy, the Colorado
   bandit, 16320
A biographical sketch of the
   life of William B. Ide,
   16844
Biography of Christopher
   Merkley, 17183
Birds, 15879
Birds - California, 17869
Birds - Oregon, 17751
Birds - U. S., 16279
Birds of the Northwest,
   16279
Birkbeck, Morris, 1764-1825,
   16528
Birkbeck, Morris, 1764-1825 -
   Bibl., 15989
Bishop, Will C., ed., 17640
Bishop, William W., ed.,
   17011
Bison, American, 15835,
   16900
Bitter Root mountains, 16760
Black Hawk, Col. - Descr.,
   17514
Black Hawk war, 1832,
   16214, 17155
Black Hawk's last raid, 1866,
   16590
Black Hills, 16261, 16887,
   17683, 17871
Black Hills, S. D. - Descr. &
   trav., 16309, 16400,
   17122, 17123
Black Hills, S. D. - Hist.,
   17525
Black Hills Expedition of
   1874, 17858
The Black Hills gold rush,
   16042, 16992
The Black hills of South
   Dakota, 17525
Black River Falls, Wis., 15848
Blackmore, William, d. 1878,
   16401
Blaine Co., Mont. - Hist.,

17290
Blake, J. A., pub., 16686
Blake's Hand-book of Colorado,
   16686
Bliss, Stephen, 1787-1847,
   15902
Bloody Knife (Sioux-Arikara
   Indian), 17705
Bloomington, Ill. - Hist.,
   16100
Blunt, Stanhope English,
   1850-1926, 17776
Board of Trade Resources of
   Colorado, 16364
Bolton, Herbert Eugene, 1870-,
   ed., 16488, 16951
Bonanza mines, Nev., 16384
Bonnie Belmont, 16219
The book of Texas, 15962
Boone, Nathan, 1782-1857?,
   17062
Booth, Mary Louise, 1831-
   1889, tr., 16580
"Boots and saddles", 16317
Borax, 17648
The border and the buffalo,
   16271
The border bandits, 16079
The border outlaws, 16079
Border reminiscences,
   17127
Boreas, Breckenridge and
   the Blue, 17733
Botany - California-San
   Diego, 17554
Botany - North America,
   16416
Botany - Southern states,
   17245
Botta, Carlo Giuseppe
   Guglielmo, 1766-1837,
   tr., 15973
Botta, Paul Émile, 1804?-
   1870, 15973
Bottineau County, N. D.,
   16104
Bottineau County, N. D. -
   Hist., 16103
Bottling machinery, 17332

5

Boulder, Col. - Descr.,
17514
Les bourgeois de la
Compagnie du Nord-Ouest,
17148
Bourne, Edward Gaylord,
1860-1908, 17140
Boy life on the prairies,
16574
Bozeman, 15829
Braddock's campaign, 1755,
16658
Bradford, William John
Alden, 1791-1858, reporter,
16861
Breck, James Lloyd, 1818-
1876, 16800
Briceño Perozo, Mario, 1917-,
17443
Bridger, James, 1804-1881,
17945
Brief sketch of Colorado
territory and the gold
mines of that region, 17864
Brigands and robbers, 16319,
16626
Brigham Young's record of
blood!, 17068
Brigham's destroying angel,
16751
Brisbin, James Sanks, 1837-
1892, ed., 15955, 15956
British Columbia, 16354
British Columbia - Descr. &
trav., 15811, 15917,
16417, 16477, 17113
British diplomatic corres-
pondence concerning the
republic of Texas, 1836-
1846, 16630
The British emigrants "handbook", 17268
British interests and
activities in Texas, 15813
Broderick, David Colbreth,
1820-1859, 17075
Broderick and Gwin, 17306
Brown co., Wis., 15848
Brown University. John

Carter Brown library,
16534
Brown's political history of
Oregon, 16064
Browne, George Waldo,
1851-1930, ed., 17850
Browne, John Ross, 1821-1875,
16124
Bryant, Edwin, 16923
Bryce, George, 1844-1931,
ed., 17526
Buffalo, 16095
"Buffalo Bill" from prairie
to palace, 16093
Buffalo Bill's life story,
16223
Buffalo Co., Neb. - Biog.,
15933
Buffalo Co., Neb. - Hist.,
15933
The buffalo in trade and
commerce, 16095
Buffalo Jones' forty years
of adventure, 16900
Building a new empire, 15892
Bureau Co., Ill. - Descr. -
Maps, 17154
Bureau Co., Ill. - Hist.,
17157
Burleson Co., Tex. - Biog.,
16780
Burpee, Lawrence Johnstone,
1873-, ed., 16989, 17251
Burr conspiracy, 1805-1807,
16490
Burriel, Andrés Marcos,
1719-1762, 17823
Burrows, Rube, 1854-1890,
15821
Butler, Eileen, ed., 16113
Butler, James Davis, 1815-
1905, 16529
Butte St. Paul, Bottineau
County, N. D., 16101

Caldwell, Howard Walter,
1858-, ed., 17260
Caldwell, Kan. - Hist.,

6

16548
California, 15837, 16190,
  16303, 16357, 16513, 16535,
  16582, 16587, 16706, 17078,
  17130, 17505, 17822, 17823
California: an Englishman's
  impression of the Golden
  state, 16899
California - Antiq., 16741,
  17265, 17621, 17622, 17938
California - Archives, 16460
California - Bar, 17607
California - Bibl., 15905,
  17088, 17789
California - Biog., 15906,
  16089, 16334, 16612, 16653,
  16862, 16879, 17354, 17427,
  17667, 17693, 17702, 17883
California - "Boom", 1886,
  17818
California - Boundaries,
  16611, 16865
California - Centennial
  celebrations, etc., 17789
California - Climate, 16633,
  17471, 17472
California. Constitution,
  16124, 17753
California - Constitutional
  history, 16833
California - Descr. & trav.,
  15823, 15883, 15886, 15890,
  15898, 15899, 15903, 15905,
  15935, 15937, 15942, 15958,
  15973, 15976, 15996, 16016,
  16032, 16048, 16055, 16081,
  16122, 16128, 16130, 16131,
  16145, 16159, 16161, 16178,
  16181, 16182, 16190, 16193,
  16199, 16200, 16202, 16206,
  16208, 16222, 16228, 16233,
  16253, 16259, 16286, 16324,
  16359, 16374, 16386, 16432,
  16434, 16442, 16454, 16461,
  16482, 16488, 16492, 16494,
  16495, 16496, 16505, 16518,
  16521, 16533, 16540, 16617,
  16623, 16657, 16668, 16682,
  16711, 16715, 16717, 16735,

  16736, 16753, 16791, 16797,
  16806, 16809, 16815, 16836,
  16837, 16851, 16863, 16870,
  16877, 16878, 16896, 16897,
  16898, 16899, 16907, 16915,
  16934, 16935, 16950, 16954,
  16957, 16963, 17007, 17022,
  17025, 17026, 17029, 17034,
  17054, 17055, 17056, 17067,
  17069, 17133, 17134, 17189,
  17214, 17215, 17243, 17244,
  17245, 17246, 17249, 17250,
  17280, 17281, 17305, 17327,
  17328, 17369, 17381, 17382,
  17383, 17393, 17417, 17419,
  17921, 17444, 17472, 17481,
  17489, 17503, 17510, 17529,
  17537, 17546, 17557, 17559,
  17562, 17567, 17572, 17585,
  17588, 17589, 17592, 17594,
  17618, 17643, 17659, 17662,
  17667, 17677, 17698, 17699,
  17700, 17702, 17734, 17735,
  17742, 17745, 17757, 17758,
  17765, 17800, 17803, 17805,
  17842, 17844, 17849, 17853,
  17854, 17887, 17903, 17913,
  17919, 17925
California - Descr. & trav. -
  Maps, 16534
California - Descr. & trav. -
  Views, 16650, 16712, 17613,
  17831
California - Directories,
  17131, 17397, 17398, 17513
California - Econ. cond.,
  16254, 16504, 17585, 17702,
  17718
California - Fiction,
  16664
California - Fruit industry,
  16194
California - Geneal., 16089
California - Geneal. -
  Societies, 16132
California - Geology, 17879
California - Gold, 17676
California - Gold discoveries,
  15808, 15837, 15966, 15976,

7

16018, 16065, 16086, 16128,
16139, 16149, 16157, 16358,
16359, 16386, 16417, 16435,
16493, 16494, 16501, 16506,
16520, 16525, 16540, 16587,
16673, 16709, 16736, 16790,
16836, 16929, 16954, 16961,
17013, 17069, 17100, 17124,
17133, 17189, 17204, 17246,
17346, 17358, 17359, 17376,
17477, 17505, 17567, 17571,
17594, 17601, 17616, 17662,
17664, 17806, 17830, 17834,
17850, 17872, 17908, 17926
California - Gold discoveries -
Fiction, 15904, 17833
California - Golden jubilee,
17296
California: her wealth and
resources, 17601
California - Hist., 15874,
15905, 15906, 15909, 15975,
16127, 16145, 16213, 16217,
16230, 16272, 16311, 16334,
16340, 16360, 16362, 16459,
16472, 16488, 16510, 16559,
16561, 16638, 16639, 16653,
16654, 16655, 16656, 16669,
16683, 16699, 16701, 16717,
16789, 16792, 16844, 16845,
16850, 16862, 16906, 16931,
17027, 17099, 17124, 17177,
17220, 17230, 17282, 17285,
17296, 17344, 17345, 17364,
17423, 17477, 17486, 17503,
17533, 17534, 17549, 17556,
17576, 17615, 17618, 17675,
17693, 17743, 17766, 17798,
17895, 17898, 17927
California - Hist. - To 1846,
16155, 16176, 16210, 16496,
16595, 16829
California - Hist. - 1846-1850,
16610, 17073, 17600
California - Hist. - Bibl.,
16281
California - Hist. - Civil
war, 17377
California - Hist. - Societies,

16129, 17639
California - History, Reli-
gious, 17712
California - Industries,
16123
California: its gold and
its inhabitants, 16836
California - Lands, 16423,
16783, 16991, 17689, 17817
California - Maps, 15947
California - Militia, 17656
California - Missions, 16160,
17054, 17206, 17302, 17496,
17827
California - Pol. & govt.,
15944, 16039, 16149, 16343,
16559, 16610, 16683, 16750,
16936, 17006, 17075, 17306,
17380, 17523, 17584, 17773
California - Pol. & govt. -
Civil war, 16015
California - Soc. life &
cust., 15969, 16018, 16071,
16388, 16521, 16955, 17286,
17336, 17403, 17756, 17908,
17928
California. University.
Library. Bancroft
collection, 17739
California, Lower, 15843,
16073, 17822, 17823
California, Lower - Descr. &
trav., 15905, 16768, 16951
California, Lower - Hist.,
15907, 16210, 16217, 16535,
16768, 17549
California, Lower - Indians,
15895
California, Lower - Mines
and mining, 17755
California, Southern,
16090, 17037, 17271, 17644,
17819
California, Southern -
Antiq., 16749
California, Southern -
Biography, 16091, 16652,
16653
California, Southern - Descr.

8

9

10

16952
Chicago. World's Columbian
  exposition, 1893.
  California, 17192
Chicago historical society,
  16069
Chihuahua (State) Mexico -
  Descr. & trav., 16476,
  17469
Childbirth, 17278
Chiles, J. B., 16926
Chinese in California,
  16957
Chinook, In the land of,
  17290
Chinook jargon - Texts,
  16456
Chipeta, queen of Ute
  Indians, 17452
Chippewa Falls, Wis.,
  15848
Chippewa Indians, 15870
Chippewa Indians -
  Legends, 17036
Chippewa Indians -
  Missions, 16800
Chippewa language -
  Glossaries, vocabularies,
  etc., 17048
Chips of the old block,
  16358
Cholenec, Pierre, 1641-
  1723, 16956
Chorpenning, George - Claims
  vs. U.S., 16196
Chronicles of the builders
  of the commonwealth, 15906
Churchill, Sylvester, 1783-
  1862, 16201
Cincinnati - Hist., 16576
The Cincinnati excursion to
  California, 16202
Circle-Dot, 16412
Citizens of Washington
  Territory, 16970
Civil engineering, 15828
Clark, John, 1797-1854,
  16665
Clark, William, 1770-1838,

jt. author, 17030
Clark co., Wis., 15848
Clarke, S. J., publishing
  company, Chicago, Ill.,
  16941
Clarkson, James S., 16698
Claudy, Carl Harry, 1879-,
  ed., 17198
Clavijero, Francisco Xavier,
  1731-1787, 16768
Clay, Cassius Marcellus,
  1810-1903, 17454
Cliff-dwellings - Colorado,
  17279
Coahuila, Mexico, 16911
Cobb family, 15990
Cochrane, John McDowell,
  1849-1904, 16102
Cody, William Frederick,
  1846-1917, 16093, 16854,
  17118
Cole, E. C., jt. author,
  16868
Collins, William H., 17565
Colorado, 16156, 16171,
  16191, 17301, 17640, 17749
Colorado - Antiq., 16506,
  16507, 16971, 17236
Colorado - Bibl. - Catalogs,
  17792
Colorado - Biog., 16005,
  16117, 16755, 17413, 17679,
  17881
Colorado - Biog. - Pictorial
  works, 17532
Colorado - Constitution,
  16267
Colorado - Descr. & trav.,
  15831, 15986, 15993, 16005,
  16030, 16096, 16148, 16171,
  16174, 16180, 16191, 16222,
  16237, 16238, 16239, 16242,
  16244 - 16248, 16251, 16302,
  16348, 16364 - 16371, 16499,
  16539, 16544, 16545, 16571,
  16586, 16603, 16616, 16621,
  16622, 16632, 16686, 16702,
  16721, 16725, 16730, 16852,
  17016, 17199, 17200, 17362,

11

13

Croffut, William Augustus,
   1835-, 16786
Crofutt, George A., & co.,
   pub., 16631
Crónicas de ayer, 15822
Crook, George, 1828-1890,
   16024, 16515, 16947
Crooked trails, 17467
Crossing the plains, 17152,
   17163
Crow Indians, 16153, 16989
Crown cork and seal company,
   Baltimore, Md., 17332
Crumpton, H. J., 16306
Crumpton, W. B., 16306
Crusoe's islands, 16071
Cummins, H., jt. author,
   17374
Cuney, Norris Wright,
   16698
Custer, George Armstrong,
   1839-1876, 16118, 16317,
   16385, 16515, 17858
Custer co., Neb. - Hist.,
   16110

Dakota, 16409
Dakota - Descr. & trav.,
   15834, 16541
Dakota - Econ. cond.,
   15934
Dakota - Hist., 15934,
   16541, 16802
Dakota - Pol. & govt.,
   17587
The Dakota Indian victory
   dance, 15952
Dakota Indians, 15939,
   15955, 15956, 16054, 16152,
   16691, 16802, 16927, 16986,
   17174, 17402
Dakota Indians - Government
   relations, 17730
Dakota Indians - Missions,
   17401, 17491
Dakota Indians - Wars, 1862-
   1865, 16150, 16264, 16425,
   16908, 16927

Dakota Indians - Wars,
   1876, 16515
Dakota Indians - Wars,
   1890-1891, 15971
Dakota land and Dakota life,
   17263
Dakota Territory - Hist.,
   16043, 16044, 16045, 16284,
   17705, 17710
Dallas, Tex., 16869
Daniells, T. G., ed., 16123
Davenport, Ia., 16106
Davis, Herman Stearns,
   1868-, ed., 16987
Davis, John Francis, 1859-,
   16125
Davis co., Ia. - Hist.,
   16481
Davis mountains, Tex.,
   17441
Day, Gershom Bulkley,
   1804-1852, 17756
Day, Henry Noble, 1808-1890,
   ed., 15894
Days of horror, 15971
Days on the road, 16744
Death Valley, Calif., 17648
Death Valley in '49, 17124
Decatur, Neb., 16361
Deck and port, 16253
The decline and fall of
   Samuel Sawbones, 17018
Del Norte Co., Calif. -
   Hist., 16002
De Milt, Alonzo Pierre,
   1831-, 16520
Denton Co., Tex. - Biog.,
   15936
Denton Co., Tex. - Hist.,
   15936
Denver - Biog., 16782,
   17413
Denver - Descr., 17514
Denver - Hist., 16782,
   16987
Denver, Northwestern and
   Pacific railway, 17862
Description de la nouvelle
   Californie, 16505

14

16909
Early days in Texas, 17101
The early days of California,
16495
The early days of my
episcopate, 16455
Early days on the western
slope of Colorado and
campfire chats with Otto
Mears, 16891
The early history of
Illinois, 16040
Early life among the
Indians, 15870
The early sentiment for the
annexation of California,
16213
Early settlers and Indian
fighters of Southwest
Texas, 17647
Early times in Southern
California, 15958
Early times in Texas,
16444
The earth lodge, 17458
Eau Claire, Wis., 15848
Ecclesiastical history of
Utah, 16189
Echo Park Dam, 17840
Echoes from the Rocky
mountains, 16205
Echoes of the past, 15976
Ecuadorian essays, 15822
The editor's run in New
Mexico and Colorado,
16180
Education - Addresses,
essays, lectures, 17388
Education - Arkansas -
Hist., 17603
Education - California,
15820
Education - Colorado,
16240, 16642
Education - Nebraska - Hist.,
16120
Education - Texas, 16283,
17015
Education - Texas - Hist.,

16974
Education in Nebraska,
16120
Edwards, John Newman,
1839-1889, 16453
Edwards co., Ill., 16528
Edwards co., Ill. - Bibl.,
15989
Eells, Myron, 1843-, 15877
Eells, Myron, 1843-1907.
A reply to Professor
Bourne's "The Whitman
legend", 17140
Egypt - Descr. & trav.,
17116
Eight hundred miles in an
ambulance, 16893
Eldorado, 17590, 17699
El Dorado co., Cal. - Biog.,
17806
El Dorado co., Cal. - Hist.,
16890
Elliot, Sir Charles, 1801-
1875, 16630
Elliott, Wallace W. & co.,
pub., 16771, 16773
Ellskwatawa, Shawnee prophet,
1775?-1834, 16346
Ellsworth co., Kansas - Hist.,
16256
El Paso co., Col. - Hist.,
16823
El Paso, Texas, 17201
Emery co., Utah, 16776
The emigrant's guide, 17269
Emigrant's guide to the
free lands of the Northwest,
16541
En route to the Klondike,
16988
English in Illinois, 16528
English language - Diction-
aries, 16842
English language - Grammar -
1800-1870, 16555
Erman, Georg Adolf, 1806-
1877, 16815
Ermatinger, Charles Oakes
Zaccheus, 1851-, 16474

16

18

Fuller, Henry Clay, ed.,
17050
Fuller, Melville Weston,
1833-1910, 16040
Fur trade, 16350
Fur trade - Canada,
16394, 16989, 17048,
17095, 17251
Fur trade - Illinois,
16827
Fur trade - Manitoba,
17404
Fur trade - Michigan,
16827
Fur trade - Missouri
valley, 16990
Fur trade - Northwest,
Canadian, 17859
Fur trade - Northwestern
states, 17541
Fur trade - Rocky mountains,
17136, 17859
Fur trade - Upper Mississippi,
17747
Fur trade - Utah, 15882
Fur trade - The West, 15847,
16195, 16286
Furnas, Robert Wilkinson,
1824-1905, ed., 17260
Furnas co., Neb., 15892

Galena, Ill. - Hist.,
16188
Gall (Sioux Indian), 17705
Galland, Isaac, 1790-1858,
16943
Galvin, J. J., jt. author,
16796
Gannon, Clell G., ed.,
17460
Garces, Francisco, 15846
The garden of the world,
16325
Gardner, Robert, fl. 1845-
1866, 17637
A gazetteer of Texas, 16572
The geese of Ganderica,
17169

Gems of Rocky mountain
scenery, 17150
Genealogical Forum of
Portland, Ore., 17778,
17779, 17780
The general, 15924
A general circular to all
persons of good character,
16916
The genesis of California
counties, 16126
Geographisch-statistische
beschreibung von Californien,
16711
Geography, 17539
Geography - Textbooks - 1870,
16258
Geological survey of
California, 17879
Geology - California, 17133
Geology - Colorado, 16721
Geology - Nebraska, 15884
Geology - New Mexico, 17775
Geology - North Dakota, 16966
Geology - Rocky Mountains,
16723
Geology - Utah, 15948, 15949,
17620, 17786
Geology - Wyoming, 17776
Georgetown, Col. - Descr.,
17514
Georgia - Finance, 17580
Germans in Texas, 17741
Germany - Descr. & trav.,
16754
Germany - Soc. life & cust.,
16754
Geronimo, Apache chief -
Fiction, 16465, 16467
Gillespie, Joseph, 1809-1885,
17035
Gilmore, Melvin Randolph,
1868-1940, 17890
Girty, Simon, 1741-1818,
16115
Girty family, 16115
Glacier national park,
16807
Gladston, W. S., 16984

20

21

Greenleaf, Benjamin, 1786-
1864, 16183
Greenwood, Grace, pseud.,
16632
Gregory, James F., 17777
Gregory, Lair H., 17410
Grenell, Zelotes, 1841-,
17756
The Grim chieftain of Kansas,
16516
Grinnell, Elizabeth, 1851-,
ed., 16647
Griset, Ernest, 16401
Grover, La Fayette, 1823-
1911, 17309
Guadalupe Hidalgo, Treaty
of, 1848, 16959
Guard, Louis, illustr.,
17687
Guerren, Charles, 16842
Guerrillas, 16263
The guerrillas of the West,
15862
A guide to the Angelus
studios collection of
historic photographs,
16769
Gulf states - Hist. -
Colonial period, 16441
Gulley, L. C., 15866
Gunn, Mrs. Elizabeth Le
Breton, 1811-1906, 16657
Gunn family (Alexander Gun,
1785-1828), 16657
Gunnison, John W., d. 1853,
16591
Gunnison Massacre - 1853,
15691
Gunsaulus, F. W., 17276
Guthrie, Abelard, 1814-1873,
16262
Gypsies, 17029

H., E. M., 17444
Hale, Horace M., 16240
Hall, James, 1793-1868, ed.,
16848
Halsey, Gaius Leonard,

1819-1891, 16673
Hamblin, Jacob, 16714,
17043
Hamilton, Henry Edward,
comp., 16827
Hancock, Henry, 16991
Hancock Co., Ill. - Biog.,
16641
Hancock Co., Ill. - Hist.,
16641
Handbook of Iowa, 15998
Hand-clasp of the East
and West, 17493
Hands up, 16269, 16270
Haney, Lewis Henry, 1882-,
ed., 17727
Hannum, Anna Paschall,
1880-, ed., 17346
Hardy, Mrs. A., ed., 16232
Harlan, Edgar Rubey, 1869-,
16431
Harney Photogravure Co.,
Racine, Wis., 15871
Harney, William Selby,
1800-1889, 17454
Harriman, Edward Henry,
1848-1909, 17538
Harrison, William Henry,
pres. U. S., 1773-1841,
16346
Hartford union mining and
trading co., 16709
Hassam, F. Childe, illustr.,
17735
Hastings, Lansford W.,
16923
The Hastings Cutoff,
16923
Hawaii - Descr. & trav.,
17039
Hawaiian islands, 15832
Hawaiian islands - Descr. &
trav., 15942, 15973, 16016,
16029, 16031, 17281, 17751
Hawkins family, 16718
The heart of the continent,
17063
Heath family, 16058
Hecker, Thad. C., jt. author,

Hunt family, 16832
A hunter's adventures in
  the great West, 16601
A hunter's experiences in
  the southern states of
  America, 16522
Hunting, 16164, 16331, 16900
Hunting - Canada, 16685
Hunting - Colorado, 16137
Hunting - Kansas, 16137
Hunting - Southern states,
  16522
Hunting - Texas, 16523
Hunting - U. S., 16401,
  16601, 16760, 17520, 17521
Hunting - The West,
  15838, 17004, 17185
Hunting for gold, 16417
The hunting grounds of the
  great West, 16401
Huntington, Charles S.,
  illustr., 17641
Huntington, O. B., 16485
Hutchings' illustrated
  California magazine,
  17204
Hymns - Chinook jargon,
  16456

I married a soldier,
  16975
Icelanders in North
  Dakota, 17737
Idaho, 16773, 17308
Idaho - Biog., 16719,
  17626
Idaho - Descr. & trav.,
  15876, 16222, 16408,
  17408, 17409, 17777
Idaho - Hist., 16060,
  16661, 16719, 17083
Idaho. Legislature,
  17083
Idaho, Col. - Descr.,
  17514
Ide, William Brown, 1796-
  1852, 16844
Illinois - Biog., 17035

Illinois. Constitution,
  15988
Illinois - Descr. & trav.,
  17268
Illinois - Emig. & immig.,
  15988
Illinois - Hist., 16040,
  17156
Illinois - Pol. & govt.,
  16962, 17135
Illinois infantry. 2nd
  regt., 1847-1848, 17286
Illinois infantry. 10th
  regt., 1861-1865, 16884
Illustrated history of
  Nebraska, 17237
In barrack and field,
  15943
In camp and cabin, 17664
In Tamal land, 15979
In the Apache country,
  16466
In the early days along
  the overland trail in
  Nebraska Territory, 16232
In the footprints of the
  padres, 17677
In the heart of the Bitter-
  Root mountains, 16760
In the Klondyke, 17334
In the land of Chinook,
  17290
In the old West, 17542
In the Oregon country,
  17437
In the Pecos country,
  16464
In the San Juan, Colorado,
  16589
The incidental history of
  southern Kansas and the
  Indian territory, 16548
Incidents of a cruise in
  the United States frigate
  Congress to California,
  16253
Incidents of frontier life,
  17253
Incidents of the life and

24

times of Rev. Alfred
Brunson, 16077
Incidents on land and
water, 15935
India - Soc. life & cust.,
17336
Indian and white in the
Northwest, 17333
Indian fighting parson,
16625
Indian names in Utah
geography, 17338
Indian relations on the
Mormon frontier, 16059
Indian reminiscence, 15967
Indian reservations in
Utah, 17703
The Indian scout, 15824
Indian Territory, 17433
Indian Territory - Descr.
& trav., 15831
Indian Territory, a
pre-Commonwealth, 16439
Indian trade, 17264
Indian tribes of the lower
Mississippi Valley and
adjacent coast of the
Gulf of Mexico, 17692
Indian war in Oregon and
Washington territories,
16072
Indian wars of the United
States, 17228
Indian why stories, 17036
The Indian's last fight,
16234
Indiana, 16252, 16470
Indiana - Pol. & govt.,
16983
Indians, 16166, 16167
Indians, Treatment of -
U. S., 15953, 17084,
17085
Indians of Mexico, 15895
Indians of North America,
15810, 15838, 15955, 15956,
16169, 16285, 16405, 16562,
16599, 16901, 17048, 17107,
17128, 17134, 17185, 17193,

17321, 17454, 17615, 17904
Indians of North America -
Arizona, 16500
Indians of North America -
California, 17207, 17477,
17865
Indians of North America -
Canada, 16394, 17095
Indians of North America -
Captivities, 16150, 16291,
16380, 16449, 16562, 16927,
16986, 17012, 17186, 17349
Indians of North America -
Colorado, 16823
Indians of North America -
Colorado River Valley, 16137
Indians of North America -
Dakota Territory, 16728,
17710
Indians of North America -
Georgia, 16185
Indians of North America -
Government relations,
16185, 17085, 17730
Indians of North America -
Housing, 17458
Indians of North America -
Indian Territory, 17433
Indians of North America -
Iowa, 16566
Indians of North America -
Languages - Glossaries,
vocabularies, etc., 17048
Indians of North America -
Legends, 16812
Indians of North America -
Michigan, 16268
Indians of North America -
Minnesota, 15939, 17263,
17264, 17492, 17836
Indians of North America -
Missions, 16393, 16455,
16956, 17167, 17302, 17333,
17496
Indians of North America -
Missions - Dakota, 17287
Indians of North America -
Missouri Valley, 16307
Indians of North America -

25

17002, 17116, 17268, 17270, 17350
Iowa - Direct., 17269
Iowa - Econ. cond., 16839
Iowa - Hist., 16172, 17062, 17289, 17708, 17746
Iowa - Pol. & govt., 16649, 17288
Iowa: the home for immigrants, 16858
The Iowa band, 15812
Iowa cavalry. 6th regt., 1863-1865, 16425
The Iowa handbook for 1857, 17350
Iowa infantry. 1st regt., 1861, 17294
Iowa infantry. 5th regt., 1861-1864, 16116
Ira, Vt. - Hist., 17368
Irish in the U. S., 17295
Ireland, John, abp., 1838-1918, 17167
Irwin, William Henry, 1873-1948, 16888
Isham, W. P., 17116
Isham, Warren J., 1863, 17116
Islands of the Pacific - Descr. & trav., 17594

Jackson, Andrew, pres. U. S., 1767-1845, 17166
Jackson Co., Ore. - Families, 17778, 17779, 17780
Jacksonville, Ill., 16847
James, Frank, 1844-1915, 16079, 16319, 16321
James, George Wharton, 1858-1923, ed., 16215, 17344
James, Jesse Woodson, 1847-1882, 16079, 16319, 16321, 16407, 16882
Jefferson Co., Col., 15974
Jefferson Co., Iowa - Hist., 16524
Jefferson Co., Neb., 16345

Jefferson Co., Neb. - Biog., 16345
Jefferson Territory, 17363
Jesery Co., Ill. - Hist., 16677
Los Jesuitas quitados y restituidos al mundo, 17556
Jesuits, 17556
Jesuits. Letters from missions, 16956
Jesuits - Missions, 16956
Jesuits in California, 17822
Jesuits in Lower California, 17822, 17823
Jesuits in Pimeria Alta, 16951
Jimeno's and Hartnell's indexes of land concessions, 16423
Johnson, Luther Alexander, 1875-, 17796
Jones, Evan, ed., 16184
Jones, Nathaniel Vary, 1822-1863, 16904
Jones, William Albert, 1841-1914, 17776
Joseph, Nez Percé's chief, 16822
The journal of a grandfather, 16830
Journal of a trapper, 17541
Journal of Heber C. Kimball, 16945
Journalism - Colorado, 16333
A journey to, on and from the "golden shore", 17559
Juan de Fuca (Strait), 16477
Juan Fernandez (Islands), 16071
Julien, Denis, 16922, 16925
Justice (Early) in Utah, 17258

Lancaster Co., Neb. -
  Biog., 17411
Land - Taxation - Texas,
  17727
The land of enchantment,
  17875
The land of gold, 16736
The land of golden grain,
  17409
The land of little rain,
  15887
The land of Nome, 17104
Land of sunshine, Southern
  California, 16055
Land tenure, 16204, 16906
Land tenure - U. S. -
  Law, 17159
Land titles - Lee Co.,
  Ia., 16943
Land titles - San Fran-
  cisco, 17867
Lane, James Henry, 1814-
  1866, 16516
Lane, Joseph, 1801-1881,
  15985
Larimer, William, 1809-
  1875, 16987
La Salle, Robert Cavelier,
  sieur de, 1643-1687,
  16491, 16628, 16994
La Salle, Robert Cavelier,
  sieur de, 1643-1687 -
  Bibl., 16628
Lassen Co., Cal. - Hist.,
  16489
Lassepas Ulises Urbano,
  16768
Last leaves of American
  history, 17895
Last rambles amongst the
  Indians of the Rocky
  mountains and the Andes,
  16166
The last voice from the
  plains, 16424
Latourette, Kenneth Scott,
  1884-, jt. ed., 16517
Latourette, Nellie Edith,
  jt. ed., 16517

Latrobe, John Hazelhurst
  Boneval, 1803-1891, 16998
Latter-day Saints in Utah,
  17483
Law - Anecdotes, facetiae,
  satire, etc., 16413
Law as a profession, 17074
Law reports, digests, etc. -
  Iowa, 16861
Lawrence, Ia., 16375
Lawrence, Mrs. M. V. T.,
  16206
Laws of the Cherokee nation,
  16187
Lawyers, 16413, 17607
Lawyers - Biog., 17074
Lawyers - Illinois, 17035
Lawyers - Texas, 17921
Lawyers - U. S., 17091
Leavenworth, Kan., 16094
Leavenworth, Kan. Board of
  trade, 16094
Lecouvreur, Mrs. Josephine
  Rosana (Smith) ed., 17007
Lee, Jason, 1803-1845,
  15878, 16766
Lee Co., Tex. - Biog.,
  16780
The Lee trial, 17009
Legends - Mississippi Valley,
  16812
Legends - Missouri Valley,
  16812
The legion of liberty,
  15859, 17017
Le Petit, Mathurin, 1693-
  1739, 16956
Le Roy, Billy, 16320
Letters from an Oregon ranch,
  17668
Letters from California,
  17383
Letters from the Illinois,
  1820, 16528
Letters of a woman homesteader,
  17673
Letters to a friend, 17243
Lewis and Clark expedition,
  16529, 16640, 16997, 17030

Louisiana - Hist. -
Colonial period, 16040
Louisiana - Hist. -
Colonial period - Sources,
16010, 17129
Louisiana - Pol. & govt. -
1803-1863, 16490
Louisiana purchase, 16640
The Louisiana purchase and
our title west of the
Rocky Mountains, 16742
Loup River, 16531
Ludlow family, 16576
Lumbering - California,
16937
Lumpkin, C. P., jt. author,
17838
Lundy, Benjamin, 1789-
1839, 15859, 17017
Lutheran Church in California,
17667
Lutheran Church in Texas,
17691
Lyon Co., Ia. County Board
of Supervisors, 16840
Lyon Co., Ia. - Descr. &
trav., 16840
Lyon Co., Ia. - Hist.,
16840

Ma vie nomade aux Montagnes
rocheuses, 17914
McCaleb, Walter Flavius,
1873-, ed., 17453
McCormack, Thomas Joseph,
1865-1932, ed., 16962
McCutcheon, J. T., illustr.,
16753
McDermott, John Francis,
1902-, ed., 16307
McDonald, Richard Hayes,
1820-, 17089
McDonald family, 17089
McGarrahan claim, 16783
Machebeuf, Joseph Projectus,
bp., 1812-1889, 16825
Mackenzie, Alexander, 17104
Mackenzie, Ronald Slidell,

1840-1889, 16023
Mackenzie district - Descr.
& trav., 17389
Mackenzie's last fight with
Cheyennes, 16023
McKinstry, George, 16997
McLenan, John, illustr.,
17336
McLennan Co., Texas,
marriage record, 16170
McLoughlin, John, 16805
Macomb, John N., 1810-1879,
1775
Mad rush for gold in frozen
North, 16390
Madison Co., Mont., 16688
Magical and sleight of hand
performances, by Arikara,
17891
Mahaska Co., Ia. - Hist.,
17384
Mammals - Oregon, 17751
Man, Prehistoric - California,
17622
Mandan Indians, 16168, 17458
The Mandan lodge at Bismarck,
17892
Mandat-Grancey, E. de.
Dans les montagnes rocheuses,
16261
Manitoba - Descr. & trav.,
15917
Manitoba - Hist., 16438,
16552
Manti, Utah - Indians,
17470
Manufacturing, agricultural
and industrial resources
of Iowa, 16839
Map of Bureau county, Illinois,
17154
Marest, Gabriel, 1662-1714,
16956
Marin Co., Cal. - Descr. &
trav., 15976, 16596
The marine climate of the
Southern California
coast, 17471
Marion Co., Ia. - Hist., 16411

32

Mexico, 15850
Mexico - Bibl., 17835
Mexico - Bound. - Texas
(Republic), 17138
Mexico - Bound. - U. S.,
17125
Mexico - Descr. & trav.,
16404, 16797, 17056
Mexico - For. rel. - U. S.,
15834, 17166, 17188
Mexico - Hist., 15907,
15916, 16278, 16538, 17486,
17898
Mexico - Hist. - Conquest,
1519-1540, 16551
Mexico - Hist. - European
intervention, 1861-1867,
16452, 16795
Mexico - Hist. - Spanish
colony, 1540-1810, 16551
Mexico. Ministerio de
relaciones exteriores,
17188
Mézières, Athanase de,
d. 1779, 16010
Michigan - Finance, 17580
Michigan - Pol. & govt.,
17587
Middleton, Christopher,
d. 1770, 16394
Midnight and noonday,
16548
Midwives, Mormon, 17278
Miera y Pacheco, Bernardo,
15844, 15880, 15881, 17821
Milan Co., Tex. - Biog.,
16780
Millard, jt. author, 16710
Millard County, Utah,
16591
Miller, George L., jt. ed.,
17237
Milwaukee - Comm., 17203
Mines and mineral resources -
California, 16701, 17572,
17745
Mines and mineral resources -
California, Lower, 16768
Mines and mineral resources -

Colorado, 17301, 17632
Mines and mineral resources -
Government ownership, 17240
Mines and mineral resources -
New Mexico - Grant Co., 16624
Mines and mineral resources -
South Dakota, 16887
Mines and mineral resources -
U. S., 17525
Mines and mining, 16539
Mines and mining - Nevada,
15856
Mines and mining - U. S.,
17602
Mining - Camps, 17602
Minnesota, 17352
Minnesota - Climate,
16013
Minnesota - Descr. & trav.,
16012, 16026, 16227, 16405,
16678, 16748, 16914, 17049,
17303, 17610
Minnesota - Finance, 17580
Minnesota - Hist.,
15954, 16564, 16660, 17149,
17262, 17573, 17609, 17625,
17836
Minnesota - Hist. - Societies,
17205
Minnesota - Soc. life & cust.,
17540
Minnesota. State teachers
college, Winona, 17261
The Minnesota handbook for
1856-7, 17352
Mission Indians of Southern
California, 17865
A mission record of the
California Indians, 17207
Missionary adventures in
Texas and Mexico, 16404
Missionary history of the
Pacific Northwest, 16766
Missions - California,
16217, 16519, 16536,
16829, 17115, 17344, 17345,
17423, 17549, 17618, 17822,
17823
Missions - California, Lower

33

The Mormon country, 16221
Mormon midwives, 17278
The Mormon question in its
    economic aspects, 17065
The Mormon usurpation,
    17275
"Mormon" women's protest,
    17551
Mormonism, 17424
Mormonism exposed, 15910,
    15965
Mormonism unveiled, 17011
Mormons and Mormonism,
    15896, 15930, 15931, 15965,
    16028, 16066, 16109, 16140,
    16141, 16147, 16205, 16221,
    16299, 16322, 16374, 16479,
    16593, 16676, 16687, 16703,
    16707, 16751, 16881, 16901,
    16996, 17011, 17039, 17063,
    17065, 17068, 17078, 17183,
    17254, 17373, 17387, 17506,
    17551, 17582, 17654, 17663,
    17745, 17761, 17784, 17815,
    17847
Mormons and Mormonism -
    Fiction, 16485, 17906
Mormons and Mormonism -
    Poetry, 16332
Mormons and Mormonism -
    Satire, 17169
Mormons and Mormonism in
    Great Britain, 16945
Mormons and Mormonism in
    Illinois, 15965
Mormons and Mormonism in
    Iowa, 17501
Mormons and Mormonism in
    Missouri, 17208
Mormons and Mormonism in
    Utah, 17079, 17424,
    17538
The Mormons and the Indians,
    15845
Morrill family (Abraham
    Morrill, d. 1662), 17235
Morse, Charles W., 17846
Morton, Arthur S., ed.,
    17095

Moshoquop, the avenger,
    16592
Mounds and mound builders
    of the United States,
    16599
Mounds of Minnesota valley,
    17492
The mountain empire Utah,
    15994
Mountain Meadows massacre,
    1857, 16593, 17009, 17010,
    17011, 17945
Mountaineering, 16050,
    16174, 16949
Mountains and molehills,
    17133
The mountains of Oregon,
    17665
Mowry, William Augustus,
    1829-1917. Marcus Whitman
    and the early days of
    Oreogn, 17140
Munro-Fraser, J. P., 16770,
    16772, 16777, 16778
The murderer's doom!! 16014
Murieta, Joaquín, 1828 or 29-
    1853, 16841
Muscatine, Ia. - Hist.,
    16867
My adventures in the Sierras,
    17908
My friend the Indian, 17107
My life in two hemispheres,
    15898
My life on the plains,
    16318
My people of the plains,
    17697
My reminiscences, 17435
My sixty years on the
    plains trapping, trading,
    and Indian fighting, 16681
My story, 17198
My travels in the land of
    the midnight sun, 16289

Nevada: the land of silver,
17420
Nevada, Col. - Descr.,
17514
The new and the old, 17336
New education in California,
15820
The new empire, 17408
The new empire and her
representative men, 16682
New France - Disc. & explor.,
16956, 16995, 17129
New Mexico, 16003, 17266,
17392, 17494
New Mexico - Biog., 16849
New Mexico - Descr. &
trav., 15811, 16158,
16180, 16287, 16371, 16730,
17126, 17175, 17391
New Mexico - Directories,
16243
New Mexico - Hist., 15922,
16272, 16341, 16342, 16538,
16849, 17430, 17451, 17798
New Mexico - Hist. -
Chronology, 17266
New Mexico - Pol. & govt.,
17523
New Mexico - Public lands,
17669
The new Northwest, 16419
New Orleans - Hist., 16490
New Ulm, Minn. - Hist.,
15971
The new West, 16003, 16032
New York. Public library,
16560
New York cavalry. 10th
regt., 17403
New York infantry. 1st
regt., 1846-1847, 16207
New York (State) - Descr.
& trav., 16313
Newberry, John Strong,
1822-1892, 17775
Newcastle-under-Lyme, Thomas
Pelham-Holles, 1st duke of,
1693-1768, 16457
Newfoundland to Manitoba

through Canada's maritime
mining, 17440
Newmark, Marco Ross, joint
ed., 17271
Newport, R. I. - Descr.,
16313
Nez Percés Indians, 17310
Nez Percés Indians - Missions,
17843
Nez Percés Indians - Wars,
1877, 16515, 16822
Nicaragua - Hist. - Filli-
buster war, 1855-1860,
16415
Nicolet, Jean, d. 1642,
16114
Nicollet, Joseph Nicolas,
1786-1843, 17611
Niles, Mich., 17756
Nine years in the Rocky
Mountains, 17541
Nome, Cape, 16556, 16647
Nome, Cape - Descr. & trav.,
17104
Nome, Cape - Hist., 17104
Nootka Indians, 16477
Nootka language - Glossaries,
vocabularies, etc., 16477
Normal, Ill. - Hist.,
16100
North America - Descr. &
trav., 16416
North America - Hist.,
17904
North Carolina - Finance,
17580
North Central states -
Population, 16144
North Dakota - Antiquities,
17686, 17893
North Dakota - Biog., 17058
North Dakota - Climate,
17619
North Dakota - Descr. &
trav., 16409, 16573,
17000, 17628, 17845
North Dakota - Hist., 16063,
16101, 16102, 16284, 16469,
16660, 16793, 16946, 17058,

17174, 17438, 17706, 17707,
17820
North Dakota - Hist. -
Sources, 16876
North Dakota - Population,
16600
North Dakota - Social life
and customs, 16606, 17531
North Dakota. State
Historical Museum, 16063
North Dakota. State Historical
Society, 17894
The North Dakota state park
system, 17462
North Pacific history company
of Portland, Or., comp.,
16784
North Platte, Neb. - Hist.,
15817
Northern California, 16193,
16851
Northern Pacific railroad,
15876, 16921
Northern Pacific Railroad
Company, 17327
Northern Pacific Railroad
survey, 17528
Northwest boundary of the
U. S., 15925, 15929,
16064, 17202, 17759
The northwest coast, 15876
Northwest coast of North
America, 16394, 16432,
16477, 16638, 16639, 16640,
16981, 17168, 17759, 17943
Northwest company, 17148
Northwest company of Canada,
16989
Northwest passage, 16394,
16477, 16731, 17168
Northwest, Canadian, 16227,
16288, 17000, 17390, 17581
Northwest, Canadian - Descr.
& trav., 15917, 16394, 16474,
16508, 16685, 16731, 17148,
17185, 17389
Northwest, Canadian - Hist.,
17558
Northwest, Old, 16325

Northwest, Old - Descr. &
trav., 17052
Northwest, Old - Descr. &
trav. - Guide-books,
17367
Northwest, Old - Disc. &
explor., 16114, 16995
Northwest, Pacific, 17759
Northwest, Pacific -
Descr. & trav., 16046, 16416
Northwest, Pacific - Hist.,
15929, 16497, 17445
Northwest, Pacific - Soc.
life & cust., 16834
Northwestern Association of
Congregational Ministers,
16455
The Northwestern Express
and Transportation Company,
16993
Northwestern states, 16227,
16315, 16921
Northwestern states - Biog.,
16784
Northwestern states -
Descr. & trav., 16784,
16989, 17325, 17541
Northwestern states - Hist.,
16784, 16980, 17171
Norton, John W., illustr.,
16693
Norwegians in North Dakota,
17438
Notes of a voyage to
California via Cape Horn,
17805
Notes on the centennial
state, 16621
Notices of the harbor at
the mouth of the Columbia
river, 15995
Noticia de la California,
17823
Noticias de la provincia
de Californias en tres
cartas de un sacerdote
religioso, 17549
Nuevo León, Mexico.
Universidad, Monterrey,

16579
Nuñez Cabeza de Vaca, Alvar,
   16th cent., 16640

Oak, 16416
Oak, H. L., 15907
Oakland, Cal. - Biog., 16656
Ocean to ocean on horseback,
   16607
O'er cañon and crag to the
   land of gold, 16809
Off the reservation, 16465
Ogden, John, 17261
Ogle Co., Ill. - Hist.,
   16019
O'Hara, James, 1753?-1819,
   16330
O'Higgins, Harvey Jerrold,
   1876-, 16141
Ohio - Hist., 17466
Ohio - Hist. - 1787-1865,
   16576
Ohio Valley - Hist., 16116
Ohio Valley - Hist. - To 1795,
   17164
Ojeada sobre Nuevo México,
   15922
Ojerholm, John Melcher,
   1858-, 17691
O-kee-pa, 16168
Oklahoma, 15900, 17160,
   17293, 17300, 17331, 17433
Oklahoma - Admission of,
   16373
Oklahoma - Bibl. - Catalogs,
   17795
Oklahoma - Biog., 16868,
   17414, 17731
Oklahoma - Bound. - Texas,
   17583
Oklahoma - Centennial cele-
   brations, etc., 17795
Oklahoma. Constitution,
   17715
Oklahoma - Descr. & trav.,
   16088, 16868, 16885, 17210,
   17299
Oklahoma - Hist., 16143, 16203,

16280, 16314, 16439, 16605,
   16759, 17509, 17688, 17731
Oklahoma - Pol. & govt.,
   17715
Oklahoma: the beautiful
   land, 16885
Oklahoma and the rights
   of the five tribes of the
   Indian territory, 16186
The Oklahoma bill, 17331
Oklahoma outlaws, 16626
Old army sketches, 16163
Old Block's sketch-book,
   16357
Old Californian days,
   17662
Old days in the old army,
   16975
An old Kansas Indian town
   on the Missouri, 17473
The old Romish mission in
   California, 17302
Old Southwest - Bibl., 17835
Old times on the upper
   Mississippi, 17184
Old trail drivers association,
   16835
Olden times in Colorado,
   16333
Oldham, Kie, 15865
Olympus, Mount, Wash.,
   17437
Omaha. Exhibition of indus-
   try and arts, 1899, 16571
Omaha - Hist., 16663, 17641
Omaha - Stock-yards, 17165
On land and sea, 17735
On sunset highways, 17249
On the border with Crook,
   16024
On the frontier, 16137
On the mission in Missouri,
   16798
On the trail of Geronimo,
   16466
On the wing, 15996
On two continents, 16036
On two frontiers, 16082
Once their home, 16802

39

One of the people, 17403
Oneida Co., Id., 17762
Orange Co., Cal., 16850
The Orderville United Order
  of Zion, 17373
Orderville, Utah - Hist.,
  17373, 17582
Oregon, 15853, 15869,
  16916, 17238, 17313, 17406
Oregon: a story of progress
  and development, 17455
Oregon - Anthropology,
  17716
Oregon - Archives, 17944
Oregon - Biog., 15818,
  16581, 16796, 17410, 17415
Oregon. Constitution,
  16857
Oregon - Census, 1860,
  17778
Oregon - Census, 1870,
  17779
Oregon - Census, 1880,
  17780
Oregon - Descr. & trav.,
  15806, 15816, 15832, 15869,
  15876, 16027, 16222, 16285,
  16296, 16423, 16408, 16432,
  16462, 16717, 16764, 16824,
  16896, 16917, 16972, 17215,
  17242, 17250, 17255, 17256,
  17257, 17281, 17307, 17314,
  17319, 17320, 17322, 17407,
  17408, 17409, 17410, 17437,
  17455, 17502, 17529, 17546,
  17589, 17593, 17665, 17668,
  17751, 17768, 17772, 17824,
  17825, 17857
Oregon - Directories, 17248
Oregon - Econ. cond., 16597
Oregon - Hist., 15877, 15878,
  15970, 15999, 16021, 16072,
  16146, 16209, 16231, 16362,
  16446, 16447, 16581, 16585,
  16597, 16638, 16639, 16689,
  16720, 16762, 16763, 16766,
  16784, 16805, 16895, 16933,
  17020, 17045, 17071, 17072,
  17120, 17171, 17283, 17298,

17311, 17316, 17348, 17445,
  17566, 17568, 17569, 17570,
  17658, 17732, 17767, 17781,
  17826
Oregon - Hist. - To 1859,
  15925, 15929, 16064, 16142,
  16290, 16305, 16497, 16517,
  16629, 16671, 16690, 16717,
  16761, 16909, 16918, 16919,
  17093, 17139, 17140, 17141,
  17144, 17241, 17276, 17277,
  17321, 17759, 17764, 17824,
  17843, 17936, 17943
Oregon - Hist. - Period.,
  17317
Oregon - Hist. - Pictorial
  works - Catalogs, 16769
Oregon - Hist. - Societies,
  17318
Oregon - Hist. - Sources,
  16640, 17642
Oregon - Indus. & Resources,
  17410, 17713, 17912
Oregon: its resources,
  climate, people, and
  productions, 17238
Oregon: its wealth and
  resources, 17768
Oregon - Militia - Muster
  rolls, 17826
Oregon, our right and title,
  17502
Oregon - Pol. & govt.,
  16064, 17213, 17312, 17465,
  17684
Oregon - Pol. & govt. -
  To 1859, 16418, 17929
Oregon - Soc. life & cust.,
  17053
Oregon. State penitentiary,
  Salem, 16920
Oregon - Statistics, 16433
Oregon, the land of
  opportunity, 17407
Oregon, the struggle for
  possession, 15925
Oregon: there and back in
  1877, 17256
Oregon. University. Dept.

of economics and history,
17642
Oregon and the orient,
16027
The Oregon archives, 17309
Oregon as it is, 15816
Oregon branch of the
Pacific railroad, 17374
Oregon historical society,
Portland, 17642
The Oregon missions, 15929
Oregon presidential
electoral vote, 17213
Oregon question, 16255,
16497
Oregon trail, 16345
Organic act of Montana
territory, 17222
Organization of the Texas
revolution, 15912
Origin and fall of the
Alamo, 16537
Orion (ship), 16886
Orleans (Ter.) Laws,
statutes, etc., 16940
Osage Co., Kan. - Hist.,
16634
Osage Indians, 16389
Oskaloosa, Ia. - Hist.,
17384
Our barren lands, 16729
Our brothers and cousins,
17098
Our country and its
resources, 16813
Our Italy, 17842
Our legacy from the Dahkotahs,
16802
Our new states and territo-
ries, 17485
Our western archipelago,
16508
Ouray, chief of Ute
Indians, 17452
Ouray (Unitah and) Indian
Agency, Fort Duchesne,
Utah, 17740
Outlaws, 16323, 16819
Outlaws of the border,

16407
Outlines of history of
the Territory of Dakota,
16541
Over the purple hills,
16200
Over the wilds to California,
15940
Overland journey to
California, 15964
Overland journeys to the
Pacific, 15804, 15861,
15897, 15919, 15964, 15976,
16007, 16286, 16295, 16296,
16308, 16388, 16501, 16560,
16594, 16623, 16631, 16717,
16723, 16744, 16866, 17004,
17019, 17020, 17063, 17080,
17096, 17152, 17163, 17171,
17175, 17218, 17286, 17292,
17346, 17394, 17405, 17522,
17571, 17751, 17756, 17936
The overland stage to
California, 17522
Overland to Cariboo, 17113
Overland to Oregon in the
tracks of Lewis and Clark,
17020
Owyhee Co., Id., 16767
Owyhee Co., Id. - Direct.,
16767
The ox team, 17171
Ozark mountains, 17574

Pa-ha-sa-pah, 17525
The Pacific coast, 16682,
17193
Pacific coast - Descr. &
trav., 16432, 16508, 16871,
16898, 17822, 17823, 17849
Pacific coast - Hist.,
16070, 16432
Pacific coast Indians, Wars
with, 1847-1865, 16608,
16834, 16942, 16953, 17826
Pacific history stories,
16070
Pacific Northwest, 15876,

17409
Pacific Northwest - Descr.
& trav., 17408
Pacific Northwest - Econ.
cond., 16597
Pacific Northwest - Hist.,
16597
Pacific ocean, 15908,
17168
The Pacific railroad, 16029,
16205, 16602
Pacific railroads - Early
projects, 16165, 16973,
17003, 17057, 17395
Pacific railroads - Explor.
and surveys, 15961, 17337
Pacific states, 16293, 17078,
17928
Pacific states - Climate,
17037
Pacific states - Descr. &
trav., 15811, 16071,
17244, 17717
Pacific states - Econ. cond.,
16073
Pacific states - Hist.,
16638, 16639
Pacific states - Pol. &
govt. - Civil war, 16936
Pacific states - Soc. life
& cust., 17602
Pacific trail camp-fires,
16933
Pacific wagon roads, 16854
Page Co., Ia. - Biog.,
16941
Page Co., Ia. - Hist.,
16941
Pahute biscuits, 17070
The Pahute fire legend,
17339
Pahute Indian government
and laws, 17340
Pahute Indian homelands,
17341
Pahute Indian medicine,
17342

Pahute Indians, 16814
Paine, Clarence Summer,
1867-1916, ed., 17260
Painter, Edward, 1812-1875,
17332
Painter, William, 1838-1906,
17332
Paleontology - New Mexico,
17775
Palmer, Sutton, illustr.,
15886
Paltsits, Victor, 1867-, ed.,
16560
Panama, 17067
Panama - Descr. & trav.,
16222, 16417
Panama - Pacific international
exposition, 16233
Pancho Villa's last hangout,
17634
Papers of the California
historical society, 16129
Paradise on earth, 16726
Paris. Exposition universelle,
1867, 15856
Parish, John Carl, 1881-, ed.,
16172
Park, George S., 17147
Parker, Cynthia Ann, 1827?-
1864, 16380
Parker, Henry Webster,
1822-1903, 16649
Parker, Isaac Charles,
1838-1896, 16700
Parker, Quanah, 1854-1911,
16380
Parker Co., Tex. - Biog.,
16781
Parker's Fort, Tex., 16380
Parker's Fort, Tex. -
Massacre, 1836, 17349
Parks - North Dakota,
17459, 17461, 17462, 17463
Parks - Utah, 17922
The parks of Colorado,
16604
Parry, Charles Christopher,

1823-1890, 17776
The past, the present and
  the future of the Pacific,
  16293
The pathbreakers from river
  to ocean, 16733
Patten, Benjamin Adam,
  1825-1877, jt. author,
  15927
Pawhuska, Okla., 16389
Pawnee Indians, 17851
Payne, David L., 1838-1884,
  16868
Peatfield, J. J., 15907
Pecos country, 16464
Peirce, Henry Augustus,
  1808-, 15984
Pelham, Henry, 1695?-1754,
  16457
Pella, Ia. - Descr., 16801
Pembina, N. D. - Climate,
  17619
Pembina Co., N. D., 17737
Pen knife sketches, 16358
Pen pictures of representative
  men of Oregon, 16796
Peñalosa, Diego Dionisio de,
  1624-1687, 16503
Pencil sketches of Montana,
  17151
Pendleton, Calvin Crane,
  1811-1873, 17370
Pensacola, Fla. - Hist.,
  16441
Peninsular campaign, 1862,
  16942
Peoria, Ill. - Direct.,
  16427, 16428
Peoria, Ill. - Hist., 16427,
  16428, 17156
Peoria Co., Ill. - Hist.,
  16428
Perforated stones from
  California, 16741
Personal memories of the
  United Order of Orderville,
  Utah, 17582

Personal reminiscences of
  early days in California
  with other sketches, 16510
Peru, Ill. - Hist., 15951
Philip Kearney, Fort, Massacre
  at, 1866, 16151, 16152, 16153
Phillips, Paul Chrisler,
  1883-, 17325
Photographs - Catalogs,
  16769
Physical geography -
  Nebraska, 15884
Physical geography - U. S.,
  16602
Physicians - Utah, 17524
Pickett, Joseph Worthy,
  1832-1870, 17553
Pictorial Oregon, 17410
A picture of pioneer times
  in California, 17872
Pictures of an inland sea,
  16968
Picturesque California and
  the region west of the
  Rocky Mountains, 17244
Picturesque Cheyenne and
  Arrapahoe [!] army life,
  16448
Picturesque Utah, 17081
Pike county ahead! 16356
Pike's Peak, 16674
Pike's Peak - Views, 16049
The Pike's Peak region,
  16245
The pilgrim and the pioneer,
  15959
Pima Indians, 16951
Pimeria, Alta, 16951
Pine, 16416
The pioneer, 17181
The pioneer campfire, 16937
Pioneer days in California,
  16149
Pioneer days of Oregon
  history, 16209
Pioneer days on Puget Sound,
  16363

St. Elias, Mount, 16050
Ste. Genevieve, Mo. - Hist.,
  17535
St. John, Percy Bolingbroke,
  1821-1889, ed., 15825,
  15827
St. Louis - Biog., 16328
St. Louis - Hist., 16197,
  16328
St. Louis. Louisiana Purchase
  Exposition, 1904, 16414
St. Louis River, 16564
St. Martin, Alexis, 1797?-
  1880, 15946
St. Paul, Minneapolis &
  Manitoba railway, 16409
The Salmon River Mission,
  17608
Salt Desert Trail, 16924,
  16926
Salt Lake City, 16229,
  16546, 17763
Salt Lake City - Biog.,
  15983, 17760
Salt Lake City - Descr.,
  16009, 16378
Salt Lake City - Direct.,
  16583
Salt Lake City - Hist.,
  17760
Sam Houston and the war of
  independence in Texas,
  17899
Sampitch Indians, 17470
Sampson, Francis Asbury,
  1842-, 17132
Samson, William Holland,
  1860-1917, comp. and ed.,
  16105
San Antonio, Tex. - Descr. -
  Guide-books, 16275
San Antonio, Tex. - Hist.,
  15918, 16275, 17932
San Benito Co., Calif. -
  Biog., 16655
San Benito Co., Calif. -
  Hist., 16655

San Bernardino county,
  California, 16850
San Diego, Calif. - Descr.,
  17554
San Diego, Calif. - Direct.,
  17554
San Diego county, Calif.,
  16850
San Fernando de Bexar,
  16283
San Francisco, 15969, 17699
San Francisco. Committee
  of vigilance, 17047, 17097,
  17534
San Francisco - Descr.,
  16358, 16374, 17666
San Francisco - Direct.,
  16944
San Francisco - Hist.,
  15927, 16068, 16445,
  16789, 17097
San Francisco - Pol. & govt.,
  16445
San Francisco, Journal of
  a voyage to, 16886
San Francisco Bay, 16421,
  16534
San Francisco Bay - Antiq.,
  17265
San Joaquin River, Cal.,
  16442
San Joaquin Valley, Cal. -
  Biog., 16656
San José, Calif. - Hist.,
  16667
San Juan Co., Utah, 17070
San Juan Co., Utah - Hist.,
  16902
San Juan exploring
  expedition, 17775
San Juan mountains, 16329
San Juan region, Col. -
  Descr. & trav., 16589
San Luis Obispo Co., Calif.,
  16775
San Luis Obispo Co., Calif. -
  Biog., 16655

San Luis Obispo Co., Calif. -
Hist., 16655
San Luis Park, Col., 16604
San Luis Park, Col. - Descr.
& trav., 15993
San Rafael, Calif. - Descr.,
16596
Sand Creek, Battle of, 1864,
16823
Sandhum, Henry, illustr.,
16870
Sandwich Islands to lower
Oregon, 16324
Sangre de Cristo, Slopes of
the, 16370
Sanpete Co., Utah, 16776
Santa Clara Co., Cal. -
Hist., 16777
Santa Cruz Co., Calif. -
Biog., 16655, 16777
Santa Cruz Co., Calif. -
Hist., 16655
The Santa Fé trade, 16636
Santa Fé trail, 16636,
16725, 17041, 17132, 17544
Sarría, Vicente Francisco,
1767-1835, 17207
Sauk Indians, 16634
Saunders, George Washington,
1854-, 16835
Savage, Charles R., illustr.,
17081
Sayre, James V., 17410
Scenes and adventures in the
semi-Alpine region of
Ozark mountains of Missouri
and Arkansas, 17574
Scènes de la vie californienne,
16587
Scenes in California and the
Sandwich Islands, 16016
Scenes in the Indian country,
17051
Scenes of earlier days in
crossing the plains to
Oregon, 16295
Scenes of wonder and curiosity

in California, 16837
Scenic Utah, 16969
Schafer, Joseph, 1867-,
jt. author, 17684
The school lands of Colorado,
16642
Schuyler Co., Ill. - Hist.,
16794
Scott, Alfred L., 1862-,
jt. ed., 17691
Scott, Winfield, 1786-1866,
16942
Scott Co., Ia., 16106
Scouts and scouting, 15941,
17224
Scraps of California history,
16844
Sculptured anthropoid ape
heads, 17716
Seals (Numismatics), 17904
Seamen, 16326
The seat of empire, 16227
Seattle. Alaska-Yukon-
Pacific exposition, 1909 -
California, 16123
Seattle - Hist., 17431
The second William Penn,
17544
The secret service of the
Confederate States in
Europe, 16085
Seeking fortune in America,
16643
Seeking the golden fleece,
17675
Selkirk, Thomas Douglas,
5th earl, 1771-1820, 17404
Semi-tropical California,
17757
Seminole war, 2d., 1835-
1842, 16458
Semple, Robert, fl. 1848,
16717
Señan, José Francisco de
Paula, 1760-1823, 17207
Separatism in Utah, 1847-1870,
16322

South America - Descr. &
trav., 15942, 16253,
16520, 17854
South Carolina - Finance,
17580
South Dakota - Descr. &
trav., 16307, 17525,
17845, 17871
South Dakota - Hist.,
16402, 16779
Southern California,
16915, 17643, 17644
Southern states - Church
history, 16838
Southern states - Descr. &
trav., 16523, 17245
Southwest, New, 15850,
16640, 17337
Southwest, New - Bibl.,
15850
Southwest, New - Biog.,
17427
Southwest, New - Descr. &
trav., 15961, 16273,
16795, 16960, 17031,
17488, 17787, 17875
Southwest, New - Disc. &
explor., 16503
Southwest, New - Hist.,
15992, 16334
Southwest, New - Hist. -
Civil war, 17377, 17378
Southwest, New - Soc. life
& cust., 15887
Southwest, Old, 16567
Southwest, Old - Descr. &
trav., 16960, 17247
Southwest, Old - Hist. -
Civil war, 17900
Southwest, Old - Hist. -
Sources, 16010
Southwestern states -
Cattle - Hist., 17086
Southwestern states -
Cattle trade, 17086
Spain - Colonies -
North America, 15992
Spain - Exploring expedi-
tions, 16477

Spain - Hist. - Historiography,
16038
Spalding, Henry Harmon,
1803-1874, 17843
Spaniards in California,
15905
Spaniards in the U. S.,
16441
Spanish and Mexican
exploration and trade
northwest from New Mexico
into the Great Basin,
16758
The Spanish archives of
California, 16460
Spanish colonization in
the Southwest, 15992
The Spanish conquest of
New Mexico, 16342
Spanish mission in
California, 16155
Spanish missions of
California, 16668, 17207,
17662
The Spanish press of
California, 1833-1844, 16282
Spanish Trail, The old,
16758
Sparta, Wis., 15848
Spirit lake, Ia. - Massacre,
1857, 17012
Spirit of adventure,
17252
Sport and adventures among
the North-American Indians,
17185
Sporting excursions in the
Rocky mountains, 17751
Stage lines in Dakota,
16043
Standing, Joseph, 17273
Star forty-six, Oklahoma,
16143
Starley family, 17655
Starring, William Sylvanus,
d. 1889, jt. comp., 16842
Stage coaches in the West,
16993
Statehood bill, 16373

True detective stories from
  the archives of the
  Pinkertons, 17216
A truthful woman in southern
  California, 17557
Tuberculosis, 17471
Tucker family, 16828
Tukuarika Indians, 15839
Tulare Co., Cal., 17689
Tulare Co., Cal. - Biog.,
  17179
Tulare Co., Cal. - Hist.,
  17179
Tulare valley, Cal. - Descr.
  & trav., 16157
Tulip female seminary,
  Tulip, Ark., 17388
Turner, Frederick Jackson,
  1861-1932, 16478, 17504
Turtle River State Park,
  North Dakota, 16966,
  17463
Twelve months in Klondike,
  16958
Twelve nights in the hunters'
  camp, 15924
Twenty eventful years of the
  Oregon Woman's Christian
  temperance union, 15818
Twenty-five years a parson in
  the Wild West, 16067
Twenty-four years a cowboy
  and ranchman in southern Texas
  and old Mexico, 17680
Twenty years among our hostile
  Indians, 16831
Twenty years in a newspaper
  office, 15842
Twenty years of detective life
  in the mountains and on the
  plains, 16269
Twenty years on the range,
  16288
The twin hells, 17480
Two summers among the
  Musquakies, 16108
Two thousand miles on horseback,
  17175
Two women in the Klondike,

16787
Two years before the mast,
  16326
Two years in California,
  16259
Two years in Oregon,
  17257

Ubique, pseud., 16601
Unadilla, N. Y., 16673
Uncle Dudley's odd hours,
  17540
Under six flags, 16337
Under the black flag, 16323
Under the prophet in Utah,
  16141
Under the sky in California,
  17562
Under the turquoise sky in
  Colorado, 17511
Union Pacific railroad,
  16398, 17019, 17337, 17476
Unitah and Ouray Indian agency,
  17740
United States, 16526, 16813
U. S. - Annexations, 17187
U. S. Army, 16448
U. S. Army. Dept. of the
  Platte, 17197
U. S. Army - Hist., 16942
U. S. Army - Military life,
  15868, 16151, 16163, 16317,
  16473, 16608, 16786, 16948,
  16975, 17031, 17060, 17102,
  17127, 17128, 17190, 17198,
  17829, 17847
U. S. Army. 2d cavalry
  (Colored), 16402
U. S. Artillery. 3d reqt.,
  1821-1901, 16953
U. S. - Biog., 17091
U. S. - Bound., 16491, 16811
U. S. - Bound. - Mexico,
  17125
U. S. Cavalry. 1st regt.
  dragoons, 1833-1861, 17060
U. S. Cavalry. 5th regt.,
  1855-, 16947, 17428

57

U. S. Cavalry. 6th regt.,
1861-, 16162
U. S. Circuit court (8th
circuit), 16700
U. S. Congress. Senate.
Select committee on the
Oregon territory, 16640
U. S. Dept. of State,
16640, 17188
U. S. Dept. of the
Interior - Archives,
16876
U. S. - Descr. & trav.,
16017, 16208, 16212, 16580,
16602, 16607, 16643, 16754,
16963, 16998, 17098, 17295,
17360, 17387, 17550, 17654,
17763
U. S. - Descr. & trav. -
1783-1843, 17194
U. S. - Descr. & trav. -
1861-1899, 17506
U. S. - Descr. & trav. -
Guide-books, 16651
U. S. District court.
Arkansas (Western district),
16700
U. S. - Emig. & immig., 17387
U. S. - Exploring expeditions,
16273, 16554, 16914, 17218,
17391, 17422, 17620, 17776,
17777, 17786, 17787
U. S. - For. rel. - Mexico,
15834, 17166, 17188
U. S. - For. rel. - Spain,
16962
U. S. - Hist., 15968, 17904
U. S. - Hist. - Addresses,
essays, lectures, 16478
U. S. - Hist. - Civil war,
15852, 16483
U. S. - Hist. - Civil war -
Biog., 16483
U. S. - Hist. - Civil war -
Campaigns and battles,
16397
U. S. - Hist. - Civil war -
Fiction, 16219
U. S. - Hist. - Civil war -

Guerillas, 15862, 16271,
16323
U. S. - Hist. - Civil war -
Indian troops, 15854
U. S. - Hist. - Civil war -
Naval operations -
Confederate states, 16085
U. S. - Hist. - Civil war -
Personnal narratives,
15868, 15941, 16116, 16188,
16298, 16402, 16458, 16525,
16679, 16884, 17046, 17137,
17190, 17193, 17219, 17403
U. S. - Hist. - Civil war -
Personal narratives -
Confederate side, 15943,
16396, 16594, 16625, 16830,
17399, 17453, 17902
U. S. - Hist. - Civil war -
Personal narratives -
Union side, 17377
U. S. - Hist. - Civil war -
Prison life, 17578
U. S. - Hist. - Civil war -
Prisoners and prisons,
16116
U. S. - Hist. - Civil war -
Regimental histories -
Cal. inf. - 1st, 17378
U. S. - Hist. - Civil war -
Regimental histories -
Colorado cav. - 2d., 17900
U. S. - Hist. - Civil war -
Regimental histories -
Ia. inf. - 1st, 17294
U. S. - Hist. - Civil war -
Regimental histories -
New York inf. - 40th,
16525
U. S. - Hist. - Civil war -
Regimental histories -
Texas cav. - 8th, 16396
U. S. - Hist. - Civil war -
Regimental histories -
Texas cav. - 26th regt.,
1861-1865, 16351
U. S. - Hist. - Civil war -
Regimental histories -
U. S. cav. - 6th, 16162

U. S. - Hist. - Civil war -
Regimental histories -
U. S. inf. - 8th, 17578
U. S. - Hist. - Civil war -
Registers, lists, etc.,
17940
U. S. - Hist. - Civil war -
Secret service - Confe-
derate states, 16085
U. S. - Hist. - French and
Indian war, 1755-1763,
16658
U. S. - Hist. - King George's
war, 1744-1748, 17176
U. S. - Hist. - War of 1812 -
Personal narratives, 15875
U. S. - Hist. - War of 1812 -
Prisoners and prisons,
15875
U. S. - Hist. - War with
Mexico, 1845-1848, 16034,
16458, 17093, 17895
U. S. - Hist. - War with
Mexico, 1845-1848 - Per-
sonal narratives, 16795,
17286
U. S. - Hist. - War with
Mexico, 1845-1848 -
Campaigns and battles,
16272
U. S. - Hist. - War with
Mexico, 1845-1848 - Naval
operations, 17477
U. S. - Hist. - War with
Mexico, 1845-1848 -
Personal narratives, 16335
U. S. - Hist. - War with
Mexico, 1846-1848, 17187
U. S. - Hist. - War with
Mexico, 1846-1848 -
Personal narratives, 16625
U. S. - Hist. - War with
Mexico, 1845-1848 -
Regimental histories -
N. Y. inf. - 1st, 16207
U. S. - Hist., Military,
17428
U. S. Infantry. 1st regt.,
17829

U. S. Infantry. 8th
regt., 17578
U. S. Infantry. 18th
regt., 1861-, 16151, 16153
U. S. Laws, statutes, etc.,
17222
U. S. - Pol. & govt.,
15944, 16962, 17785
U. S. - Pol. & govt. -
1815-1861, 16463, 17087,
17764
U. S. - Pol. & govt. - 1829-
1837, 17166
U. S. - Pol. & govt. - 1841-
1845, 15833, 17799
U. S. - Pol. & govt. - 1849-
1877, 16649
U. S. - Pol. & govt. - 1854-
1872, 16230
U. S. - Pol. & govt. - 1865-
1898, 17087
U. S. - Pol. & govt. - 1909-
1913, 16487
U. S. - Pol. & govt. - Civil
war, 16542, 16580, 16942,
17087, 17145
U. S. - Pol. & govt. -
Handbooks, manuals, etc.,
17684
U. S. Post office dept.,
16196
U. S. - Posts and forts,
17008
U. S. - Public lands,
17159, 17788
U. S. - Territorial expansion,
17093
U. S. Utah Commission,
17079, 17815
U. S. - War of 1898 -
Regimental histories -
U. S. cav. - 6th, 16162
The United States and the
British Northwest,
1865-1870, 17558
The United States consulate
in California, 16931
The United States of
yesterday and of tomorrow,

15926
Universities and colleges - Colorado, 17021
Universities and colleges - Nebraska, 16120
An unsophisticated exposition of Calvinism, 16074
The uprising of a great people, 16580
Untold tales of California, 16513
The unvarnished West, 17400
An unwritten chapter of Salt Lake, 1851-1901, 16707
Ups and downs of an army officer, 15868
Utah, 15994, 16410, 16881, 17550, 17771
Utah, Admission of, 17907
Utah - Antiquities, 17636
Utah - Bibl., 17110
Utah - Bibl. - Catalogs, 17791
Utah - Biog., 15983, 16299, 16334, 16429, 16479, 17626, 17761, 17762, 17846, 17856
Utah. Board of trade, 16803
Utah - Centennial cele-brations, etc., 17791
Utah - Church history, 16189
Utah. Constitution, 16429, 17809
Utah - Descr. & trav., 15809, 15847, 15896, 15910, 16198, 16221, 16222, 16229, 16371, 16374, 16378, 16410, 16687, 16803, 16996, 17081, 17170, 17173, 17387, 17424, 17506, 17620, 17771, 17786, 17801, 17847
Utah - Descr. & trav. - Views, 15872, 16969
Utah - Descr. & trav. - Year-books, 17810
Utah - Directories, 16243, 17811, 17812
Utah - Econ. cond., 16486, 17065

Utah - Geneal., 16479
Utah - Hist., 15809, 15847, 15882, 15930, 15931, 15932, 16140, 16147, 16304, 16312, 16322, 16332, 16334, 16350, 16592, 16659, 16675, 16703, 16707, 16708, 16714, 16751, 16864, 16889, 16904, 16913, 16922, 16923, 16924, 16925, 16926, 17039, 17042, 17068, 17110, 17173, 17230, 17234, 17254, 17258, 17450, 17637, 17638, 17655, 17663, 17682, 17736, 17761, 17762, 17782, 17821, 17840, 17846, 17855, 17880, 17907, 17923, 17945
Utah - Hist. - Period., 17813
Utah - Hist. - Sources, 15846, 16004, 16590, 16747, 17608, 17942
Utah - Maps, 15844, 15880, 15881, 17821
Utah - Militia, 17426
Utah - Pol. & govt., 15991, 16141, 16811, 16913, 16939, 17079, 17275, 17483, 17538, 17548, 17551, 17784, 17809, 17815, 17816
Utah - Pol. & govt. - Hand-books, manuals, etc., 16429
Utah - Pol. & govt. - Satire, 17169
Utah. State prison, Salt Lake City, 17273
Utah - Statistics, 17808
Utah Indian slavery, 17638
Utah Indians, 17343
Utah State Association of County Officials, 17810
Utah State Historical Society, 17813
Ute Indians, 16891, 17340, 17452, 17470, 17638

Valdés Flores Banzán y Peón, Cayetano, 1767-1835, 16477
Van Buren Co., Ia., 16375

60

Vancouver island, 16477,
17168
Vasquez de Coronado,
Francisco, 1510-1549,
17563
Velez de Escalante,
Silvestre, fl. 1708-1779,
15844, 15846, 15880, 15881,
17821
Vermilion Co., Ill., 16226
Vickers, William B., 1838-,
16782
Views and descriptions of
Burlington & Missouri
river railroad lands, 16098
Vigilance committees,
16392, 16980
Vigilance committees -
Louisiana, 15911
Vigilante days and ways,
16980
Villa, Francisco, 1877(ca.)-
1923, 17634
Vincennes historical and
antiquarian society,
Vincennes, Ind., 17001
Vincennes, Ind. - Hist.,
17001
Virginia - Descr. & trav.,
17902
Virginia - Finance, 17580
Virginia - Hist., 16218
Vivien, Louis, 1714-1756,
16956
Vizcaino, Sebastian, 1550?-
1615, 17823
Voorhees, Luke, 16997
Voyage au pays des mines
d'or, 15889
Voyage dans les solitudes
américaines, 16405
Voyage in a six-oared skiff
to the Falls of Saint
Anthony in 1817, 17049
Voyages and travels,
16158, 16326, 16567, 16886,
17653
Voyages around the world,
15973, 16228, 16981, 17040

Voyages en Californie et
dans l'Orégon, 17546
Voyages made in the years
1788 and 1789, 17168
Voyages to the Pacific coast,
15921, 16145, 16253, 16657,
16709, 16736, 16886, 17007,
17477

Waage, Chris M., ed., 16417
Wabash Valley, 16470
Waco Baptist Association,
Texas, 17838
Waiilatpu, its rise and
fall, 1836-1847, 16142
Walker, Joseph R., 16926
Walker (Yawheraw), Chief of
Utes, 17470, 17855
Wallace, Frederick T.,
16501
Waller, Edwin, 1800-1883,
17365
The war in Texas, 17066
War-path and bivouac, 16515
Warner, Edward, 17324
Wasco Co., Or., 17053
Wash-A-Kie, chief of the
Shoshones, 17678, 17901
Washburn, John Davis,
1833-1903, 16421
Washington - Hist., 16072
Washington (State), 16484,
17172
Washington (State) - Descr.
& trav., 15869, 15876,
16408, 17182, 17408, 17409,
17824, 17825
Washington (State) - Hist.,
16041, 16363, 17032, 17431
Washington (State) - Pol. &
govt., 16834, 16970
Washington territory, 17182
Washington (Ter.) Legislative
assembly, 16484
Washington Co., Id. - Hist.,
16705
Washington Co., Neb. - Hist.,
15960

61

16493

What I saw on the old Santa Fe trail, 17041

What I saw on the west coast of South and North America, 15942

What the poets have found to say of the beautiful scenery on the Denver & Rio Grande, 16369

Wheeler, Christine Gordon. Along the road to freedom, 16277

Wheeler, Esther W., jt. author, 17868

Le Whip-poor-will, 16021

Whipple, Amiel Weeks, 1818-1863, 17218

Whitaker, Robert, 1863-, 17020

White, Elijah, 15832

White, James, 1863-, 16474

White Pass and Yukon railway, 16627

Whitman, Marcus, 1802-1847, 16062, 16142, 16290, 16355, 16671, 16690, 17139, 17141, 17241, 17276, 17277

Whitman, Mrs. Narcissa (Prentiss) 1808-1847, 16142

Whitney, Asa, 1797-1872, 17395

Whitney, Orson Ferguson, 1855-. Popular history of Utah, 15932

Who conquered California? 16845

Who's who in Pacific south-west, 17883

Why a rich Yankee did not settle in California, 15890

Why our flag floats over Oregon, 16671

Why we went gypsying in the Sierras, 17029

Widney, Joseph Pomeroy, 1841-, 17037

Wild bats sowings, 16316

Wild life in Oregon, 16764, 17857

Wild life in the far West, 16795

Wild sports in the far West, 16588

The wilderness hunter, 17521

Wilkins, James, ed., 16701

Wilkinson, James, 1757-1825, 16490

Willamette River Valley, 16977

Willamette University, 16762

Willett, F. C., pub., 16686

Williams, C. Scott, tr., 17344

Williams, Ezekiel, fl. 1807-1827, 16286

Williamson, John, 1822-, 17082

Williamson Co., Tex. - Biog., 16780

Wilson, Hiero Tennant, 1806-1892, 16609

Winkler, Ernest William, jt. ed., 16892, 17722

The winning of the far West, 17093

Winslow, Richard H., d. 1861, 16983

A winter in California, 17903

Wisconsin, 16985

Wisconsin (Territory), 17612

Wisconsin - Descr. & trav., 16012, 16648, 16678, 17268

Wisconsin - Hist., 16648

Wisconsin - Hist. - Period., 15848

Witchcraft, 17173

With fire and sword, 16116

With rod and line in Colorado waters, 16545

With sack and stock in Alaska, 16050

With Stevenson to California, 1846, 17073

With Sully into the Sioux land, 16693

With the border ruffians,
17902
Withycombe, James, 17437
Woman - Biog., 16057,
16299, 16875, 17229
Woman - Legal status,
laws, etc., 15944
Woman - Suffrage, 17783
Woman's Christian Temperance
Union. Oregon, 15818
A woman's reminiscences
of six years in camp with
the Texas rangers, 17498
Women as physicians, 17856
Women in Confederate States
of America, 17774
Wonder-land illustrated,
17284
The wonderlands of the
wild West, 16147
Wonders of the Sierra Nevada,
17421
Wood, F. T., illustr., 16083
Wood, Myron W., 16770
Woon, Basil Dillon, 1893-,
16119
Worcester, Samuel Austin,
1798-1859, ed., 16183
World's fair ecclesiastical
history of Utah, 16189
Wraxall, Sir Frederick
Charles Lascelles, bart.,
1828-1865, tr., 15824,
15826, 17687
Wyeth, Newell Convers,
1882-1945, illustr.,
16223
Wyoming, 16468, 17366,
17769
Wyoming - Bibl., 17797
Wyoming - Biog., 15928
Wyoming - Capitol, 17937
Wyoming - Descr. & trav.,
15809, 16852, 17683, 17754,
17769, 17776, 17777, 17871,
17941
Wyoming - Directories,
16243
Wyoming - Hist., 15928,

16153, 16175, 16475, 16732,
16826, 17180, 17197, 17783,
17797, 17841, 17937
Wyoming - Land, 16175
Wyoming - Libraries, 17432
Wyoming - Pol. & govt.,
16475, 16732
Wyoming valley, Pa. - Hist.,
17366

A year of American travel,
16553
Yellowstone Expedition,
17860
Yellowstone highway, 17941
Yellowstone national park,
16722, 16979, 17284, 17429,
17776
Yellowstone national park -
Descr. & trav., 17092
Yellowstone national park -
Guide-books, 17941
Yellowstone valley - Descr.
& trav., 17092
Yesterday and today in
Arkansas, 15893
York, Lem A., ed., 17541
York factory express journal,
16474
The Yosemite, 16087
Yosemite valley, 16200,
17572
Yosemite valley - Descr. &
trav. - Views, 16650
Young, Brigman, 1801-1877,
16140, 17011, 17068, 17761,
17945
Young, Frederick George,
1858-, 17072, 17642, 17936
Young, Samuel C., 16923
Young Co., Tex. war, 1857,
17191
Younger, Cole, 1844-1916,
15862, 16079, 16407
Younger, Henry Washington,
d. 1862, 15862
Younger, James Henry, 1848-,
15862, 16079

64

Younger, John, 1850-1874,
   15862
Younger, Robert Ewing,
   15862, 16079
The Younger brothers,
   16052
The Youngers' fight for
   freedom, 16052
Yukon River and Valley -
   Descr. & trav., 16727
Yukon territory, 17251
Yukon territory - Descr.
   & trav., 16727

Zimmermann, Erich Walter,
   1888-, 17571
Zimmermann, Margaret Hoff,
   17571
Zoology - North America,
   16164

ILLUSTRATORS

Andrew, John, 17687
Anthony, A. V. S., 17336

Beard, J. C., 17520
Blood, Isabelle, 16047

Dixon, Maynard, 16082

Farris, Constance, 16048
Frost, A. B., 17520

Gifford, Fannie E., 17520
Gifford, R. Swain, 17520
Greatorex, Eleanor, 15805,
  16632
Griset, Ernest, 16401
Guard, Louis, 17687

Harmer, Alexander R., 17484
Hassam, F. Childe, 17735
Howard, Oscar Frederick,
  17031
Huntington, Charles S.,
  17641

Ivins, William S., 16866

Keeler, Louise M., 16915

Longmire, J. M., 17932

McCutcheon, J. T., 16753
McLelan, John, 17336
Mathews, Alfred E., 17150,
  17151
Meek, E. Nora, 16899
Merrill, Frank T., 16082
Morgenier, R., 17020

Narjot, Ernest, 16482
Norton, John W., 16693

O'Neill, Rose Cecil,
  17906
Orr, J. W., 17905

Palmer, Sutton, 15886
Piercy, Frederick, 17387
Prittie, Edwin J., 16467

Remington, Frederic, 1861-
  1909, 17193, 17468, 17469
Russell, Charles M., 16818

Sandham, Henry, 17520
Sartain, John, 17905
Sartain, Samuel, 17905
Savage, Charles R., 17081
Smith, E. Boyd, 15887
Stellmann, Louis J., 17666

Telfer, R., 17905

Weir, Harrison, 16588
Wells, William L., 16818
Wetherbee, F. I., 16493
Williams, Waldo, 17441
Wyeth, Newell Convers,
  1882-1945, 16223